PREFACE

To all my readers I ask for your forgiveness. The information from my aging dad, is not one continuous read, since as we talked, some forgotten areas of his life could be remembered, as he spoke of another. To be frank, I chose to take all of his valuable memories in whatever order he chose to give them.

Shortly after these inter recordings, my father passed on, making these pages even more valuable. I ask for your tolerance.

This books first chapters are the events lived by a proud black man..Waiting for the breakdown of Prejudice and hate presented to his family during the early parts of his life until the end. It is to honor His mother, who chose to defy the social rules of where a woman's place was, and instead, reset the Legacy of family on a path she through would lead the generations of the new Nichols clan to a self Respecting successes. To become proud of the path set forth for the new generations to set the expectations even higher that those set by her, for the future of the grand children, and their children. I regret that I have only the words of her son for this writing..

NOTE. Record any one of your family while you still have them in your mist. Do it, do it now !!

ZBOOK

CHAPTER 1

According to his mother on November 30, 1922 a young baby was born named VERNON HARVEY

NICHOLS. To a Mississippi Negro household in a little town in Mississippi, daddy Joe, mother Mary Craig, and two brothers. It was said that back in time Negro people had nothing except what was given to them by their owner. Joe is – helped on a farm raising harvesting tobacco, while Mary the kids, the chickens, the pig and one cow stayed home during the day, doing those motherly things cooking cleaning and looking after the kids.

I'm the son of a man, the subject of this book ,about a young man I really never knew, and a family history. In the later years of his life after the loss of his wife, my mother, he stayed in my home and gave me the opportunity to learn things that I never knew possible from my father. Most of the information from here on will be about dad, from the recorded voice of my father's life and his comments.

Daddy, from now on I'm going to turn on this tape machine, to record what you say. You can answer my question any way you chose, as long as you want…. Is that okay? "OK " . Start talking first what you remember as a young boy. Well, I remember living in running and playing with the other kids about my age one little younger, I know that nighttime, just about the time to go to bed we always heard the train clanging and banging, hooking up train cars and people talking, we were that close to the tracks, actually trains were in the area so close, it would shake the house, mama had to hold down some of the dishes that were on the shelves. It was really dark in the neighborhood so much so that the single streetlight down on the corner was the only thing you can see at night, and that's why mother made us all be inside the yard when the sun went down. As young as I can remember we were always told that when the police came through checking on the neighborhood if we were out by the curb we could go to jail, that scared us to death nobody wanted to go to jail, we heard about a neighbor boy who went to jail and the white boys didn't, jail really messed him up, when he came out he never said much... kept to himself, and one day there was a gunshot everybody heard, where he shot himself, in those days things would happen, but the older folk, would not tell the children anything, so we had to ease drop while they talked on the front porch to find out what happened. I remember the lady we were staying with her name was Beulah, and she and my mother both worked at the laundry all day and sometimes half the night. Beulah's husband would stay home with us during the day while we played in the yard and down the street where a house had been torn down; with all the stuff cleared away; it was a perfect place for us to play ball. Seems like we were always dirty and dusty, cause every night when mother would come home they made us take a bath, I'm told that water was not that good quality anyway because it was always boiled first before it was poured into the bathtub and mixed with cold water, never really understood that, but as I said, little children were not told much about anything, we were just told do it and shut up., days dragged on it seems like each day took a million years while we were children, but then finally school started I believe the school's name was Dunbar.

I remember many hours when school was not going on we would go down to the hollow, as a matter of fact now it's been called rattel bone hollow. As kids eavesdropped on older folk, I remember them saying that slaves who had escaped from the south would hide down in hollow, until they can find their way further north. There was a river and I remember an area called Quindaro, and those people over there were all white people, and they wouldn't cross the river where you know you just did not do that, white and Negro were always separate. When we started school, I remember part of our family had to go to another school, the Craigs, they were related to my mother through her mother, but they were white. Soon they all moved to another part of town, and we only saw them on holidays and special events. I might add, just as a side note, that they moved over to the Huron area near Grandview Boulevard, and that was only two blocks away from waterway Park, the only park where League Negro baseball could play back in the 30s, and adjacent to the property owned by Mattie Fields: you might remember that name as your great grandmother's name on your mother's side. Although when I was young I had no idea that the two families would ever be connected in any way. Anyway back to grade school, I think one of the names was called Dunbar elementary school. Most Negro schools were named after some famous Negro man, that was supposed to give us hope for the future. I won't bore you with the details of grade school but we all hoped to get to high school and junior high school because there was a brand-new set of schools built just for the colorards. In those days just to have a school that wasn't in a barn are just out in the weeds was considered to be an accomplishment for the race.

About that same time your grandmother my mother met a gentleman named Jefferson, he took my brother and me in, and we moved to 2315 N. 5th St. now let me remind you that that is only a few blocks away from Qundarol Avenue and the Quindaro drugstore. That was the place where if we had the night out we would stop there and get a soda or grandma's STOMACH meds or the pills that she had to take. It had real stools and a soda fountain and real soda jerk, that's the kid that wears all white white hat that makes you drinks with soda pop ice cream. All the neighborhood all hung out there on those hot summer nights believe it, in Kansas we had some hot summer nights. That reminds me of the store on the corner in the other direction, to buy chewing gum and some canned goods so grandma would not have to go all the way to the grocery store, 10 miles, you know there were no large grocery stores anywhere in the Negro neighborhood. Excuse me but my memories start and I remember things I had not remembered for years, let's get back to Mr. Jefferson. After he married my mother, things started to change. He actually started talking to RJ my brother your uncle, about manly thing things that a mother just doesn't know to teach their sons; like how to do a handshake how to look another man eyes to eye or how to count money. More importantly he had a car and he knew how to drive so now RJ and I really wanted to learn how to drive, sometimes he would let us drive down the block to the drugstore, very slowly, so everyone could see us driving. That's when RJ, who was a few years older than I started looking at girls, he would sneak them in the back yard under the grape vines, and kiss them, I remember I thought that was terrible, little did I know that soon I would want to do the same thing.

I hate to jump around that is, I talk I remember things like Grandma Craig. That was my mother's mother. After a while she appeared in the house and began doing most of the cooking while Mary my mother started working at a fabulous new job, they said on the front porch as the evening was going, that she had now left the laundry and was working for VFW, no I didn't know what that meant, but I did knows that she joined some organization named something star; and after that joining our lives started improving. later I found that this star was a woman's group connected to the Masonic Masons. You see in those days women of any color really did not have much status they were just there to make babies to cook and take care of the home so my grandmother was considered to be kind of uppity we kids did not know what that meant but my mother constantly told me and my brother always try to look out for your neighbor and your friends and always try to do everything better than your best, if you do that whenever you work with you will be on top and maybe just maybe somebody might notice how good you are and maybe just maybe your generation may see the value and the quality of black men in this country. We listened to this speech over and over again especially when we did something that wasn't quite right in my mother's eyes we got that speech either before or just after we got a lashing with the local switch, of which we had to go out and get..... such a crime that was to get punished with a stick that you had to go get so we learned pretty quickly, not to get one of the switches off the tree that was fresh and green because those would sting and would spring back to strike you again right on your buttocks, and they hurt, so you look for a dry twig so after about three strikes on your butt it would break and of course mother would be tired then and would give up beating on us so that meant punishment was much shorter. Bananas.... I mentioned earlier Mr. Jefferson he had a totally different view, I don't remember what he did for a living but he was a Mason and he had a car and in our neighborhood not many black men had cars so obviously RJ and I had to learn how to drive a car. Most of my friends thought we were really on top of the hog, I as it was said, because our house had a car and a short wave radio, that mother made us listen to the British and other countries news and most importantly the classical music that was broadcast late at night. You see she knew we knew how the gut bucket blues sounded because across the street from 2315 was a tavern which played the jukebox so loud and, it put the speakers outside of the Tavern on Fridays and Saturday nights so all could hear and know that if they wanted a good time with some loose women and some fast music that was the place to come. But directly across the street from the Tavern was a Pentecostal church, which soon began broadcasting their music on the biggest speakers I've ever seen placed on top of the church, and when the church was in session the band and the drum and the saxophone and the trumpet, not to mention the minister trying the same bellowed out the sounds through the neighborhood. So so they became a war between the blues and the old spiritual, so without trying we learn many songs from the blues and from the spirituals, it just depended on who we were trying to impress that we hummed the song or the tune that we thought they would enjoy. Such was the beginning of our training on how to survive in the open world or the job world as grandma called it. To get my job down the street at the pharmacy

Delivering pills, to some of the sick people. I knew that when a lady came in to order something and she had a diamond encrusted cross on the front of her black dress, that when I delivered to her house on my little bicycle it meant that I would hum some spiritual like the old rugged cross as I delivered her medicine and got her signature and many times I would get a tip because the lady would say... yes I can still find Christian boys working that help your mother so here's a 5 cent tip, now I know that if I offered my grandson a nickel tip, they would take it but they would look at me like I was crazy today's kids, it has to be two quarters up to a dollar or more, enough to make anything **happen,** but back then in 1933, a one nickel was like gold and it would buy so much candy I can't tell you how long we could make that last. Now that you have me talking, I got to remind you that the candy choices that we had was not very many, like peppermint stick I think there was a licorice there was a type of chewing gum it was in a round ball oh yeah, and there was taffy but not much else at least not in our neighborhood but we did not care it was something sweet and it was something forbidden so we would hide it in our big dungarees and sneak it in the house. We thought we were the first kids to have to do this but somehow mother knew looking back now I know she smelled it so it was best to get to grandmother first because she would help us hide, it but we had to pay her some of the candy, a small price to pay for such a delicious treat that we could have before dinner. Well let me not belabor that age because it seemed like every day was about the same, only some days stuck out particularly the day that the nuns, came to our school there was about 12 of them and they came from one of the local Catholic churches. The principal of our school and most of the teachers assembled all of the students in the gymnasium which was the largest place in the school to hold a meeting. Somehow I remember that to be around the late 1930s. I recall the topic was about young Negro boys, girls. It appeared that not only were we being told that we were not respected in the community, but we were being told what we should become as the years went on, one of the nuns said little black boys should try to become good workers to help our society and were always welcomed to come up to the Catholic church and help the fathers cut the grass and paint the church any Saturday we wanted and the pay would be having the good gracious of the nuns and being respected by the local government in the area. When school was over, I went home and casually told mother, at the table for dinner about the nuns and what they said. I had never seen my mother react in this way. She stood erect quickly from the table glaring at her mother, who also lived with us ya know, saying you see all of those church people seem to have the same lowlife idea, and I don't want any of them coming around my children again. Tears started to flow from my grandmother and my mother's eyes, RJ and I did not understand what this was about, but we were told to excuse ourselves from the table and go to the back room where the coal bin for the coal furnace was kept. As I recall this was a Friday and every Sunday grandmother would go to church and from church she would always bring some elder, preacher or official of the church home for dinner, I also recall that whenever someone from the church came to dinner they always took the favorite child pieces of chicken on their plate. Seems like they didn't care what we wanted or liked it was just what they wanted and grandma forbid us to speak up and say anything, as we picked at the dreaded white meat of the chicken that we did not like so after a while we hated Sundays, but now the rule had been spoken by my mother, Mr. Jefferson's sat there saying nothing, a wise man it seems, and from that Sunday on RJ and I could fight over the drumstick and the wing with no resistance from anybody at the table. We always had fresh fried chicken corn beautiful mashed potatoes and peas. But for the first time no preachers at the table. Quite frankly Sunday dinner became a joy from that point in my life except sometimes one of our cousins would come over named Joe Massingale. Did I mention that our schools were separate but equal, that is to say are part of town had teachers principles and even janitors that were all Negro. The only time we saw anybody that was white was when the police came to the school, to look over some of the young men who they thought had committed a crime in town the following our previous days. Whatever the age of the person that did the crime was those boys would be called out to the gymnasium and we would stand there while several white people would walk down the line of kids staring into our eyes and looking at our clothes, to see if we were the ones that did the crime. As I recall they never told us what the crime was but we would miss class and stand there for an hour or so while the police and these strange looking people would give us the eye. Sometimes they would pick two children out of the group and dragged him away screaming and crying, I often wondered where those the people that committed this unknown crime or did they just have to pull someone out to blame them for whatever this was the maybe they didn't do. It was the beginning of our community or at least me realizing that some of the fears that my mother had told us about, from the old days of living down south may be coming to our little place in Kansas. During those same years I remember the parades that would be in the streets less than one block away from our house, a parade of people and drums playing and a parade and the sign in front of them said America for Americans, and everyone except the band had on little white uniforms that looked to me like goblin sheets with a pointy hat, that looked like a dunce, yes son I know you know what they were but we didn't at that time. The police would be in the front of the group and the police would be behind the group until the parade had cleared the streets and our new traffic lights that had just then installed in our neighborhood. If you're not clear out today you it was the beginnings and, shall I say the ending of the public KKK, the crew clucks clan. Usually someone in our neighborhood would always tell us if you see one of them run and hide because if they are in the neighborhood something bad is going to happen. As I recall every year during summertime there was this parade same people same police front and rear but there were no black people along the curb anymore, what grew where the numbers of white faces that cheered the group as they walked down the street, this sounds impossible I'm sure now but then it was the way it was.

"Well dad what did they do about it, couldn't they make them stay out of our neighborhoods. If we were supposed to have some…. you know privacy" no son,,,, you see nothing that we had was ours, so we were told. so we simply had to grin and bear it, in fact Mr. Jefferson once told me that things are better than they were, and hopefully as you boys grow up, it will get better and better and better. At that age we really didn't know what that meant, we just went back to playing and going to the sock hops in the school and looking at the young girls, one of which was this girl that lived down the street with her parents. I finally got to know who she was when we went to the segregated high school named Sumner high school her name was Adams; Nanthalyne Adams. I thought what kind of name is that, and how do you spell naphthalene. I made it my business to know, and actually I started playing basketball because that's the only sport that the girls could stay late after school to watch us play, and no… I was not that good. I tried out swimming class but that was no fun because we could not wear swimming trunks, we found out later that the school district thought that Negroes carried unbelievable diseases, so we were required to swim in the nude. The Sumner high school building was the first high school for Negroes in the Kansas City area. So the new administrators actually allowed a special board of education for the black schools or, Negro schools,..Oh I FORGOT THE Mexican schools in Argentine, they too were totally separate from the white schools. Our Superintendent was named Mr. Lewis, a little short man seemingly very educated, but never spoke loudly are shouted at anyone. I later learned that he was chosen just because it was thought he would not raise any issues; with no white superintendent leadership, he would just vote away they wanted him to vote and besides we had a new high school, so why would we want to complain about anything. There was one teacher that stood out that I remember, she was young and an English teacher guess what her name was, yes it was Miss. Bloodworth, that tells you something because as I recall she was your English teacher too; that's how long she was there, seems like she would never never go away but she made it very important that we learn all the classics, and learn how to speak properly, and learned how to walk, hold our heads up high, and even how to laugh. It wasn't clear then, but it is now, that she and the other teachers were placing us on a highway of success. We didn't know then that the image and the speech that we brought with us from the South would be a bad thing, that our personal experiences and food types was considered a bad thing. I soon learned that when working at the local gas station, wiping the windshield and placing gas in the car, if I spoke nice and white, I can usually get a tip from the owner of the car. No longer was a simple church hymn reason to gain a tip, I had to learn how to say yes sir and yes ma'am to anybody that was white. In fact sometimes when I was not having a good day and I forgot to say yes sir, we would be penalized by not getting our days pay.

If you'll let me I'm going to jump way ahead, like through high school, which was a real boring place for me. The only things I remember I enjoyed was singing on the front steps, playing basketball, and trying to see under the girls skirts, as they climbed the stairs in front of us. That brings us back to your would be mother, did not know that then, but her mother was name Pearl, and she would come every day walking and pick up Nat and her sister Shirley and walk them home. Damn I never had a chance to get close to her, and if I did, the younger sister Shirley would always start crying, that made the people along the way home look at us and think that we boys had done something wrong, and even though they did not know us people, they would come to their porch and holler you boys get away from those girls and leave them alone. Why would they say that.

After many small jobs, I knew, that eventually with the war going on; that my best chance to be a man in my community would be join the army. Seven weeks of training in Texas, we were assigned to the Tigers, a group of heavy truck drivers in the Negro brigade.. Then on to the southern part of the US, boarding the big big queen MARY boat to Europe...twenty days later..We saw land, the coast of France

After we got there on this big boat I've never seen the most dreaded hum, so many people, but we finally landed. Got off the boat; and the first landing remember was France, of course we stayed there a couple days, oh! I don't think I remembered before this detail you have not heard, when we first got drafted, you know I was in Texas, at a training army base. There all month and a half I think. We were to learn how to drive and service big army trucks, that was my my my duty assignment was driving gigantic trucks.They taught us how to drive, change oil, replace the engine, we learned motor stables. The big trucks had speed limits on the motors. The underground, rumor mill, said we would just carry cargo. We finally left Texas, next time we talk; I'll look up where that was in Texas, the school the truck army school in Texas. When we left there,

NEGRO WWII TRUCK DRIVERS

I was told or we were assigned to the tigers; and that we will be driving munitions. We did not know what munitions were. Gorgeous , we were glad to have the trucks and not rocket launchers. being fed the meals, being paid…and we were doing our thing, you know patriotic, and and we thought that by the time we got back to the states, we would be like every other respected American, regular citizens, you know like everybody…. everyday Americans, even may help me get a job and all that, so we were currently excited about it, finally we got our us truck license, we started moving around in Germany, up in the northern part near Bremerhaven, and all that. Then we received a wake-up call by my commander OUR commander was weird and white. All the rest of

us were called then, the Negro brigade, so those of our historical writings, but the truth is, that we had to pick up these long cylinders, some in these boxes, that were over us on this hoist, some larger than the biggest car we had seen. They had some of the guys out there with forklifts, all white; we were forbidden to drive them. We had a little younger servicemen orderly type person, he was black too. They rode as copilots, in case we needed to have ground guide, somebody to help with backup, that's what he was for; but they forgot to tell us that these munitions that had been dropped by some of our allied bombers, and that they didn't go off, I mean they did not explode.....YET then they told us, but beware!! If you drive over too many potholes trenches and stuff; because we don't know why they didn't go off, and they could go off at any time. While that may be just great just imagine it is like to drive in a gasoline refinery, and when you're driving through this area, everybodys smoking cigars. The pleasure of driving well, frankly son, I was scared as hell half the time, most of this work, especially when we would drive at night, around some of those trails that were barely wide enough of donkey, truckers in one line, one direction going around curves up and down the mountain, all that and you may have some big bumping, or you hear the stuff rattling and clanging in the back; and and you wonder is this thing going to go off. once we were doing that for about a month now, one time we were on the trail going somewhere, don't remember where it was but, it was nighttime , heading back to what were going to be camped out or bivyac for the night, and one of the trucks in the line blew up. It lit up the nite sky, it was about five trucks ahead of us, maybe 50 of us driving, and it just blew up. Anilarated the truck, driver co driver, and I think it even took out some trucks in front of it. We had to stop, but we also had to get out of the area fast. Cause if any German patrols were in the area, surely they saw the explosion. And and then we took one of the trucks behind the burning ones, and just pushed it off the road. So they would roll down the mountain, couldn't stop for any remains, even if there were something to find; you know, and now, we where a big target, because the the fire in the
 Night sky, in case some of the enemy might see, it's always a chance of that. And it did happen a couple times with those German troops would shoot at us. Yes, these things that honestly,, I didn't tell you about, I know you're looking at me, wondering, you never told you some things,, things, well things, that bring back such bad memories, serves up bad visions that a man really don't want to remember anymore, you loss people that you knew, and and you thought that maybe (tears streaming down his wrinkled cheeks) of those, the bad things I really want to not remember the bad thing so, I have a tendency just not to mention them. To feel depressed so. So to recall, the good part of the job was the stops, some of these towns in France, aware we were traveling, then so anyone in the town would notice we were mostly Negros, and you know the rumor about negro men... these girls all ran after us, they wanted to have you come to their place, and they were all white girls, white, French , they would seek us out because, they thought the rumor ,perhaps that the black soldiers were better and romance making, you know!! So that was a good thing because forbidden the United States where we come you you you did not look at anybody that was not your race. So this to us, we were in heaven, and some of these places where it had been bombed and abandoned is up for grabs, and the commander took the best un-boomed house for HQ, usually the cellar had wine, it was loaded and soon the commander was loaded too. He let us drink and let us have a good time, sometimes just for one night. So that's another part I

couldn't tell you. You were younger and because now, you are older, and now you

know, the father could not go around telling his young adolescent child about things like that, now I can laughingly say some of those things I remember. some of the times not all the time but sometimes, when there were no bombs to haul, we had to guard German prisoners; prisoners of war that had been captured, and so we have to guard some who continued and attempted escape. The funny thing that we quickly noticed, was they will be in a tent, and have a fence around them, and they would have to have our guns out, especially at the gate, and guard at the fence, walked the fence, you know for guard duty and everything, but when it was time to eat, some of the MPs (military police)white soiders, would come to help us. They were to help. So we marched the Germans down into the nearby town. We marched, left right ..links & rex, down a restaurant, they would go inside these buildings to eat. Some times we had more than 40 prisoners with only a few guards, we would have the guard stretched, because we go into say 10 different eat houses, you know to take care of all the people. Geneva conventions say prisoners must be fed, at least one hot meal daily. They were snittchel and warm potato salad. WE WERE OUTSIDE IN THE COLD WEATHER RAIN WHATEVER IT WAS, and WE HAD THE K RATIONS RATIONS THEY THEY GAVE US THEN THEY WERE PERMITED, CANNED, MOSTLY COLD SOMETIMES THEY LET US WHILE AT the back of THE RESTAURANT, PUT OUR CANS ON THEIR FIRE, that would AT LEAST warm the SPAGHETTI in a can, OR THE WHATEVER WAS IN THE CAN, BUT WE THOUGHT THAT THIS WAS ODD, WHERE THE PRISONERS WERE EATING BETTER THAN WE WERE, STILL BOTHERS me EVEN TODAY I THINK ABOUT THAT IS we're WERE GIVING SERVICE TO OUR COUNTRY, BUT ABUSE WAS OUT OF A CAN. We NEGRO MEN WERE NOT ALLOWED INSIDE THE EAT PLACES. After they enjoyed their hot dinner, we would gather all of the GERMAN PRISONERS, AND WALK THEM BACK UP TO CAMP AND make sure THEY HAD WATER in their CANTEENS, AND THEN WE GO TO BED SLEEPING USUALLY OUTSIDE, AND IN A SMALL TENT, WHILE THEY SLEPT IN THE BIG Quonset tent, complete with wood stove. OCCASIONALLY THERE WAS SOME ODD THINGS HAPPEN.... AND LET ME TAKE A BREAK HERE..ok ?   one evening I had my mail...one was a box from my mother, inside was big rolled up newspaper..one prisoner was waving his hands towards me... HE WAS A GERMAN PRISONER, Summoning WAVING HIS HAND AT ME. I WAS READING THE PAPER THAT MY MOM SENT ME; YOUR GRANDMOTHER SHE WAS 70 ish then... THE KANSAS CITY STAR FROM KANSAS CITY SOMETIMES IT CAN BE TWO WEEKS OLD BY THE TIME WE GOT IT, BUT IT WAS STILL FROM BACK HOME YOU KNOW WHEN YOU OUT THERE BY YOURSELF hearing bombs in the distance ,feeling the next bomb ONE COULD BE YOU old newspapers are REALLY VALUABLE. Anyway; I WENT OVER TO THE FENCE AND WHEN I GOT THERE I REMEMBER SAYING what is lose my BEST ATTEMPTED SPEAKING GERMAN; AND THE GUY SAID, can I SEE THAT PAPER AND I SAID PAPER ? YOU SPEAKING ENGLISH I said. HE SAID YES I SPEAK PERFECT ENGLISH AND HE DID. THE ENGLISH IS BETTER THAN MINE.
 I THOUGHT HOW DO YOU KNOW HOW TO SPEAK ENGLISH. HE TELLS ME THE STORY THAT HE WAS ACTUALLY FROM CHICAGO, AND HAD TRAVELED OVER

TO GERMANY TO VISIT SOME OF HIS ANCESTORS , like his GREAT GRANDPA in

1938, AND WHILE HE WAS THERE THE WAR STARTED , THIS WOULD BE ABOUT
1939 I GUESS AND SO WELL, WHEN THE GESTAPO CAME AROUND TO GET
YOUNG ABLE-BODIED MEN FOR THE WAR YOU DID or YOU were killed. If you said
to THEM THAT YOU WERE AN AMERICAN. YOU WERE dead, so YOU JUST
MARCHED ON DOWNSTAIRS, AND AND WENT in TO WHEREVER THEY
INDUCTED young men, YOU GOT A HAND STAMPED, AND GOT PAPERS AND
THEY STUCK YOU WITH A NEEDLE OD MEDS IN YOUR BUTT, AND SO, HE
FOUND HIMSELF IN THE ARMY FOR GERMANY. THERE WAS LOTS OF PEOPLE
LIKE THAT, BUT THEY DIDN'T SAY A WORD, ABOUT WHO THEY WERE they
SPOKE THE LANGUAGE, went TO THE TRAINING,BUT YOU KNOW IN THEIR
HEARTS THEY REALLY DIDN'T WANT TO FIGHT; ESPECIALLY IF THEY'RE
SHOOTING A GUN OR SOMETHING .SHOOTING AT THEIR FRIENDS FROM BACK
IN THE STATES , SO OBVIOUSLY WHEN THE FIRST OPPORTUNITY CAME TO
THEM TO TO GIVE UP, up GOES THE ARMS TO surrender , get CAPTURED THEY
DROPPED their WEAPON, TO RAISE THE ARMS UP, AND IF THEY WERE LUCKY,
AND MOST OF THEIR LITTLE GROUP WAS SMALL ENOUGH WHERE THE OTHER
PART OF THE GROUP WOULDN'T SHOOT THEM FOR GIVING UP, or BECOME
SABOTEURS, THEY WOULD SURVIVE TO BE AND KEPT as pow, UNTIL THE BIG
ARMY WHICHEVER IT WAS, FRENCH OR AMERICAN or EVEN RUSSIAN, THEN
THEY WERE OUR ALLIES YOU KNOW,COULD CAPTURE HIM UP, AND TAKE
THEM TO AN allied NATO PRISON CAMP, SOMEWHERE, SO GOING BACK TO
STATES. HE TOOK MY PAPER, REALLY ENJOYED IT; WE GOT TO BE KINDA
FRIENDS IN A WAY, AS MUCH AS I COULD. NEXT HE WANTED ME TO GET A
MESSAGE TO HIS FAMILY. THAT WAS RISKY. IF HE WAS A SPY I COULD GET
SHOT OR I COULD BE ARRESTEDBUT SHOT. SOMEHOW HIS BLUE EYES JUST
TALKED ME INTO IT, HE LOOKED , HIS SEMI-TALK TO ME LIKE I WAS
SOMEBODY, SOME OF OUR COMMANDERS DIDN'T TALK TO US, WITH THE
UTMOST RESPECT SO, HE SCRIBBLED A MESSAGE, THE NEXT TIME WE HAD
TIME DOWNTOWN SOME OF THE BARS AND SOME LADIES, I TOOK A CHANCE
AND I GAVE THAT MESSAGE WITH AN ADDRESS TO ONE OF THE LADIES DOWN
THERE; THAT I MET A COUPLE TIMES AND AND AFTER WHICH HE DID THIS
MESSAGE TO THESE PEOPLE, YOU SHOULD'VE SEEN THE LOOK ON HER FACE,
BUT SHE DID; THANK GOD SHE DIDN'T TURN ME. I WOULD'VE BEEN
CONSIDERED A SPY, OR WORSE. EVENTUALLY A NOTE CAME BACK, SAME
SOURCE TOOK ABOUT TWO WEEKS AND THESE PEOPLE AMBLED THEIR WAY
UP THE MOUNTIAN; THEY TALKED TO THE COMMANDER. THEY APPARENTLY
THEY GOT ENOUGH TRUST FROM HIM THAT THEY WERE ALLOWED UP THE
HILL, AND GOT A CHANCE TO TALK TO THEIR RELATIVE, THAT WAS GERMAN
PRISONER, I NEVER QUITE FIGURED OUT HOW THEY DID THAT, UNTIL THE
SECOND TIME THEY ARRIVED THESE GERMAN FOLK HAD A PACKAGE, FOR ME,
SOMEHOW THEY WERE NOT CONSIDER A THREAT. THEY GAVE ME A
PACKAGE, AND IT WAS TOO SMALL REVOLVERS AND ONE OF THE GERMAN
WILDERNESS GUYS, WRAPPED UP IN A BIG BLANKET, AND SHE EXTENDED
HER GRANDMOTHER TYPE ARMS TO ME. TO SAY THANK YOU FOR GETTING

THE MESSAGE TO THEM. THOSE ARE THE THE ONES WRAPPED UP IN MY

dresser. I KEEP THEM THERE; THAT'S THAT'S WHY THAT'S THERE, THEY CAME FROM; YOU KNOW IN THOSE DAYS WE CAN BRING BACK THINGS LIKE THAT NOBODY REALLY REALLY CARED, SO IT BECAME ONE OF MY MEMORABILIA RELICS.THAT BRINGS BACK SLOW-MOTION MEMERIOS FOR ME. I NEVER TOLD ANYBODY THAT I DON'T KNOW. IS IT STILL TOO LATE, CAN I GO TO PRISON NOW, FOR BRINGING BACK SOME OF THE FRUITS OF WAR. I DON'T KNOW, I'VE ALWAYS BEEN AFRAID OF THAT BUT, NEVER SAID MUCH ABOUT IT, LEFT IT ALONE, BUT, YOU TOLD ME YOU WANTED ME TO BE TOTALLY HONEST, SO THAT'S WHAT YOU ARE GETTING, TOTALLY HONEST.... THE WHOLE TRUTH AND NOTHING BUT THE TRUTH. I'D LIKE TO TAKE A BREAK NOW... IS IT OKAY... JUST A SHORT BREAK.

well dad would you like to start this again, okay okay great what do you want to know, just start where you left off you know back when you did not tell me everything about the guns you know: well as I recall that was the highlight of the time that we spent near this big town in Germany I think it was Bremerhaven our something like that the next big thing I remember was a little town in Würzburg Germany, and there was a bar that had been bombed, they moved the bar and all the drinks and the wine below ground , basement. For more Space, but one of the things that I liked is this big curved bar went around the whole room almost, and GIs could sit down and carve messages in short letters to their girlfriends back home but it would cost you I think a nickel something like that, so of course you know that I carved your mother's name in there with a knife, something like I love nanthalyne, I was really surprised

When you wrote to me and told me you had found that scratching in that bar in Würzburg. I began crying, fortunately I was on watch that night working as a firefighter in Kansas City so no one saw me but, it was a very hard night, crying, to realize that life and history had gone full cycle and now my son was in the same place where I had been years earlier. I am sure the reason why you found it so easily is because your mother's name is very unique, NANTHALYNE...

I suppose that's about the only thing I remember that was good about the time that I was in the service, that tied us together. but the time that you were in Southeast Asia and of course Germany. I know that we were really afraid, your mother and I, when we discover that you were not only in Germany or Europe, that you were also in Southeast Asia. We did ask around a cousin we thought that if you are single surviving son that the military would not put you in harm's way area where you could be killed, at least that's what the rules said. But your grandmother Mary said you were different sort of person, than I was in the service, and probably you had volunteered to go. So when we found out that you had volunteered to go, actually we were quite angry, but still proud just the same. In fact that's where most of our gray hairs came from after we determined, that you were not only in Europe, but God knows where else on the world . Getting back to my war .....the days, and then weeks into months seem to go by so slowly, we we wanted to be home, back in Kansas City, we wanted to see our good friends, and

sleep in a warm bed where I can hear my grandmother frying bacon and making biscuits, and inviting me to breakfast on that sunny warm mornings in Kansas. It wasn't long, actually weeks , that we found our way on a big boat once again, on our way back to the United States. I can't tell you how I felt, most of the men in my group on the way back we separate ourselves at night, to a corner of our little sleeping area, where we silently cried with thankfulness that we had survived, God knows that many of my friends that I remembered in basic training, in Texas, that sailed the ocean with us to France, then drove through Germany, and some of the other areas that were no longer with us. It's hard now for me to remember the names, but so easy for me to see the faces of these young guys that had come from other homes just like mine, but were not to go back to their homes like we were. The one story that I just remembered that I forgot was, the one about the chaplain. I remember we were under fire from the enemy, the Germans, were shooting at us from the top of a hill, but first let me say we had been hanging around the mess hall tent to get something to eat, and it was very quiet so, it seems like whenever it was quiet the chaplain would appear, and he would walk around and with his Bible and and he would talk to us. One of the lines he would say all the time; is that we should pray, we should be hopeful and, we should be thankful. He also stated if ever there is a situation where you're in danger and you are afraid that you might be injured shot of killed. Remember that we have the shield, and he would hold up the Bible, and wave it around so that we can all see, and he asked us to believe and let the shield protect us. Well then after that, somehow we were discovered by a German platoon, they started shooting at us, the metal bullets would strike the metal pots and pans of the mess hall everybody got to the ground, and the chaplain, and his driver, immediately ran for their Jeep. Starting the Jeep they quickly made a U-turn and off they went down the dusty road, way and out the little road mountainous strip of muddy road and one of my friends, that was in our Negro brigade managed to stand up by side a tree, and he shouted to the chaplain, come back come back, you took the shield bring back the shield. Even though our lives where before our faces with bullets flying all around, you can hear the roar of laughter from the battalion commander, the platoon and some of the other men as we scrambled to get below or behind any kind of shelter we had... we still laugh about that, whenever I talk to some of the survivors of of opportunity on the phone, that's one thing we can never forget. I tried telling that joke to the Rev. of your church here in Seattle, but... I don't think he thought it was funny. Well jumping ahead again, back to the boat, we soon reached the dock in New York City, we passed by the Statue of Liberty, then this island mass, don't remember what it was called, but we can see American made cars. No jeeps no tanks just people milling around on this ferryboat that was going past us, with kids and women, that I mentioned women, of course I did, staring up at this big huge boat that all of these military people were out on the deck on the rails, hanging over waving whatever we had in our hands. Even thou it warms my heart to recall that we were back home, back to the US. Some of us openly cried, because you know, men are really not supposed to cry. Then it was the long trip on the train to get back the Kansas City, it seemed like it took longer on the train to get home, than it did to sail across the ocean, which I might add is a lot of days on water, on the waves up and the waves down and the wind and the rain and the uncertainty ; will this thing get us home or could we be sunk in the middle of this great wide water ocean as I recall, it was scary especially to the men who had never been on a boat, much less to another country.

Mary Jefferson MOM) and girlfriend Nanthalyne Adams

But finally we got home; it was 1943, my family my mother and my girlfriend was so glad to see us and the food... we had was just wonderful I, mean, real food, I mean food cooked by the hands of people who knew how to cook. No frozen peas corn okra coming out of a can lightly salted and boiled in water served on a tin plate with the bread that smelled like the very can that it came from. I mean we may have to go out tonight to get some fried chicken or my favorite catfish, and you know the kind of cooking that you grew up with, with your grandmother loving to be at the stove, and loving the looks on our faces as we consumed everything that she put on the table, not to mention the blueberry pie, I guess I better stop ...laughing....., here because I'm getting hungry.

The happiness soon left us, as soon as we removed our uniforms, which we wore them almost every day for about two weeks. During this time whenever we walked downtown, there were pats on the back, smiled and well-wishers telling us thank you for serving and more. But as you know all good things must come to an end soon, later it was too soon for us, when I was walking downtown with my mother uniforms were off, we were now in plain clothes, and some guy walking down the street wanted me to step off the curb to allow him to pass. Of course with my newfound patriotism, and belief that now we can now be true men and citizens, since we had projected our lives and our hopes and to the democracy called America, but it wasn't to be so, when the younger white man said hey, don't you know Negroes are supposed to get off the sidewalk to get out of our way. I was so angry and refusing to move off the sidewalk, I stepped up ready to punch his eyes out. But my mother in her infinite wisdom grabbed my arm and told me, it's okay sugar it's okay. I recall the long walk home in the ride on the bus of course sitting in the rear section. Although in Kansas City it really wasn't required, and there was no sign on the bus, that told us we had to sit in a certain section. It was thought or expected that if you lived there, that you knew your proper place, and you respected the other people of your race, as to not make trouble for them. Now you must remember, that I've been away from the city dodging bullets, martyrs, and enemy snipers: even though I didn't have my shield: to protect us from those flying pieces of metal.

Let me mention another important part of my life as a man as a soldier and now, as a father because, in June 1945 my wife and I had our first son, Vernon Junior. Everybody in the family on both sides, seem to carry flags of joy, because on your mother's side; on my wife's side, there had not been a male child born and almost 2 generations. So obviously they, seem to be forefront in spoiling our first son with all kinds of gifts, baby beds, wagons, , you name it: you had it. This was the first time that the other side of our family or my family which had passed, and were known to be white; actually came over to our part of town to visit, and to play with my male child. Also for the first time, I was receiving many tips from the elderly members of all sides of both families, of how to raise a child, or in the words of your great grandmother how are we going to raise a white Negro. I know that sounds funny now, but in those days, anyone that had a child, who was light skined, was considered to be fortunate. It was thought that if you were light, you would have more possibilities of success, a happy life because you were closer to blending in the status quo, or those that had power or, those that would have power in the future. In that day all Negroes had hopes of better things, freedom, jobs, and money to live a life for them and their children, that would far exceed anything that black folk had ever imagined, ever happened in their lives.

NEWLY WEDS Vernon and Nanthalyne Nichols 1944

As you grew as a little baby, we stayed at my mother's house. Out in that area of Kansas City that was called rattle bone hollow . Officially it was called when QUINDARO , and so as history shows just across the way from where we were living on fifth Street, and the QUINDARO area and the Indians name us, was another county, which very rich Jewish people lived, and as it was said, part of the Underground Railroad came right through that area. In close circles, and at times when no one was listening,

The conversations on the front porches and at the city park at family gatherings talked about this very often, as some of our family and some of our friends of our families had actually escaped their bondage years earlier, from the South, as they use the Underground Railroad to migrate further north from the southern states.

Being back in Kansas City, at home, I was still considered to be a lofty black American as was, my brother RJ who, had also joined the military too, and had decided to stay in the military, and make it his career. As many brothers we did not agree on anything. So he continued to be a soldier, and I went looking for work. Every day I was reminded by my mother ,and other members of the family, you got a boy now so you got to work, and you've got a bring him up right. I had various jobs from a local milling company, I worked at Griffin wheel foundry, those are the guys that make the wheels for railroad trains, you know those big metal things that go on railroad train. Then I got a real good job at Owens Corning Fiberglas and about that same time your mother and I purchased our first house, on Oakland. It was a duplex and the family next door that rented from us, named Kitchen, had a young son named Billy. Billy had a developmental problem, and really although he was a big guy, his age mental, never exceeded more than nine years old. But, he became your favorite play buddy, simply because he was right next door. In 1951 or so, the neighbor next door told us of an opening at the General Motors assembly plant, down in Fairfax. That was considered to be a really good job at the time for any Negroes, that really wanted to work hard, and I did. If you worked there, they helped you build and buy one of the autos you made. As I recall we bought our first car right after we bought the duplex. It was a 51 Chevrolet green notch back. Your mother learned how to drive, because she would take me to work early in the morning, and keep the car all day, so that she could take you to your grandmother's while she went to work as a seamstress, making bowling shirts. She and your aunt Shirley had great jobs during the war, at the Pratt and Whitney plant, making engines for the US Army bombers. But as all things happen, when the war ended so did the jobs, especially the women, since all of the men now were returning. In those jobs were reserved for men that returned from the war, and that meant now, many women were expected to get pregnant and have babies. My mother Mary had left my blood father when she moved up to Kansas from Mississippi. For years I thought that my father had ran away on my mother but, it was to be many many years, before I would discover that actually it was the other way around. Mama had high hopes for us, what would become her children's children, could become better than the past Negroes. She thought that it would be best, if she left to go to a more progressive area of the world to raise her children. So on the freight train RJ Vernon and Mary, traveled on the rail line until RJ, got so sick, that she had to get off. And as I'm told, that just happened to be in the train district of Fairfax Kansas. As the story goes, she walked up the big Quandaro Hill on a cool evening. Getting about halfway up the Hill, not knowing where she was going to sleep, or where we would sleep. then a lady up shouted down to here, from about 15 stairs up from the red brick road... hollered down to her, , now where is you going I'm told my mother shouted back I'm going to my house at the top of the hill. The lady, whose name was Beulah, shouted back,, you ain't going up there who you know with house up there, because no coloreds live up that high on the hill. So... come on up here and bring those kids with you. It was to be that we would live there for a year, my mother would work in the same business that Buehler was an, which was the laundry. Now mother never told us all the details except for some reason, she had a boyfriend, named Mr. Jenkins. And shortly after meeting him, we moved up the top of the hill on fifth Street, and our own house, a few years after that we moved down to the middle of Kansas City Kansas, on a street called Oakland.

Now you have to remember some of these facts are kind of old for me, and may not be totally accurate, but, I remember Mr. Jenkins died and left us a house. So while I was in the military mother had no one except her mother, who moved in to help her with bills, cleaning and cooking. that was your grandmother Craig, and the white other side of the family, which everybody knew or at least thought they were white. So now I'm back from the service and I married, have a child, have a good job at BOP plant, that's Buick Oldsmobile Pontiac plant. And my mother marriage ended, she was a member, of the I think they called it the rising Star. Space in any case that organization was the the ladies of the Masonic Lodge. Her new boyfriend was Mr. Ewing, a real dark skinned man, and a high-ranking member of the local Masons; don't remember what number it was: but he was pretty high up there.

In about 1956 the city of Kansas City, had a chance to get a large sum of money from the federal government, that would be used to buy new firetrucks, and build some new fire stations throughout the city. But one of the provisos was, that some of the men who were firemen and policemen, had to be Negroes. For the next four years are so, the city recruited several Negro staff for the fire department, the police department, and the city work crews to fix the streets, and clear the snow during the winter. I don't have all the facts, but shortly after 1959, the city was to purchase new fire trucks, because the ones we had, the law trucks were given to the city from Europe and were used, that is to say they were not new. And of course the old fire houses and trucks were given to the part of the city with the most minorities, Negroes and the Mexicans, oh , and don't let me forget the poor whites. So once again in order to get the new fire engines, and the money for the new equipment for law enforcement, the city was forced to integrate the public servants. In those days the powerful Negroes in the city always belonged to the Masons and since my mother was the girlfriend of one of the top Masons: guess what. They apparently needed some fresh drivers to help integrate the department, and my lucky break, I had certification from the federal government, US Army, that I was a truck driver, covering several different sizes of vehicles. So came the dream job offer. I can join a different section of the fire department and be one of the first truck drivers ever to drive a truck like that, for the city. We were so happy until we discovered that instead of having all of the Negro firemen at two stations, that were located in the black neighborhoods, that we were to be dispersed throughout the Wyandotte County, city of Kansas City fire departments. That actually meant one Negro for each fire station in the city. Un-be known to me, this was to be worse than my time in Europe and the service. Most of the fire department at that time. In Kansas City were people that were of Slavic background. There was lots of talk about they were pulled a tip some men I can't spell it, but it's a kind of bread that a lot of Slavic's would make for their families. My mother, never let me forget that this was a job that was only for white men, and white people would love to have, but I had it, and I had to support that son born , and this would be the best way to do that.

The working shift for a fireman was at that time, four days on, and two days off. So we slept at the station for at least three nights and prepared our food in the kitchen, and Tire groceries in the refrigerator. I quickly found that there was only one section in the refrigerator that I was allowed to have my groceries. It was in the crisper section down below. I actually remember the name of the frigid air was a shell the Nader can't spell it but I remember it and there, I kept all my sandwiches bread and everything that I was to eat including soup. But because of the hate of some of the people that I was working around who were white, I soon found that many of my sandwiches had been tainted with human waste, and by T or Kool-Aid always had a strange smell which resembled urine. Of course I reported this to the chief, who simply told me this is a new thing for many people you're just going to have to grin and bear it. Many times I really wanted to take a weapon and just hit everybody in the head in the station and then walk out catch the bus and go home. Once again my mother Mary, seem like she could tell when things were going bad because, she would come down to the station on the bus and would spend several hours with me outside the fire station consoling me, and helping me understand my place for the advancement of colored people had to be there this was my place my time to take a step up for our children for our community. Hell I remember saying why does it have to be me, there's lots of other Negroes why can't they do it. But as it is, I guess I was chosen, and he was to be me, to be all alone in that environment.

You may remember son, that many times in the summer, you were required to ride your bicycle all the way down to Fairfax from where we lived on Oakland, to bring me my lunch every day during the summer. I know from your complaints that you thought that was just crazy. But the real reason was the only way that I could have a healthy lunch and dinner, was to have someone bring my food in daily. I found out later after talking to many of the other black firemen that we got to know, that everybody had the same problem throughout the city and had their families friends etc. bring them food in lockboxes that were not perishable that could stay out side sometimes are in the kitchen with a lock on it that cannot be tampered. No, I didn't tell you that either. Because at the your time, and how you were thinking this would only cause you to have hate for anybody white, and if you remember you had just gotten about two friends that were white poor but white, and I really thought that to you might start growing hate inside for different people especially the young ones, that were your age and really should not be judged by the older prejudiced.

That kind of behavior continued for several years and those of us that were members of the integration, just kept my mouth shut and waited for the day that we could improve that. Even Mr. Ewing who was responsible for me actually getting the job suggested that we be happy where we were and look forward to the next jump in rank. Actually I thought that this was the top we would never go any higher but was grateful, that my son could see me at least in a decent job, where when I came home I didn't have to leave my greasy glass infested clothing out on the front steps to keep their dangerous chemicals away from you. Now I don't want you to forget that my mother your grandmother from the very first when you were a baby, always reminded us that we had to be a different kind of Negro, as she called it a white negga, she used to say. I really never understood what she bit until one day, we were sitting on the front porch at the house on Oakland, you remember the one that was partially built and we purchased and moved into it in about 1960. I think it was our first year living there in the yellow house on the hill and you and your friend, were cutting grass for the older members of the neighborhood that couldn't cut their, although you never really wanted to do it it was something that we just did to make our neighborhood look good. As my mother had taught me you always take care of the neighbor on either side of your house, and if everybody did that in the whole neighborhood, then the whole neighborhood would remain clean and neat, and so it was. You probably don't remember one of the boys stayed on the corner in the summer time with his aunt, Mrs. Anderson. You know the **big** white house on the corner. Mrs. Anderson was the sister of Haley family. One of the Haley went on to become the first black senator, for the state of Kansas. His brother Alex, stayed in the military for his career, and it was his son who during the summer stayed at the Anderson house and you played with him in the neighborhood sometimes. This block on Oakland was an interesting block because everybody that lived on this block was black are as we said then Negro, and had a job that was supposed to be the upper crust of the Negro community. Down near the one end of the block we had a postman who was third in command for the local postal offices and then we had several other people who were executives that the call paper, the Negro paper in town, then there was Mr. Lewis, who was the Negro superintendent of schools and across the Street from Halo of course was the teacher of the music department for the greater Kansas City schools at least the Negro portion of the schools, that was allowed by Mr. Slagle, FL Slagle as I recall was his name he allowed for the black schools are the Negro schools to have their own separate board of education, you know the old phrase separate but equal. But let's go back to sitting on the front porch of the Anderson home on the corner while you listened to Alex Haley read from little notes and scripts that he had from his travels, talking about his family. Little did we know that in years to come, that Alex would have a book written, read, and made into a movie. That movie as you remember was called roots, and became a bestseller and a highly rated movie about Negro culture. That was about the same time that you ask me where was your grandfather, or where was my daddy. I never knew that listing to someone else's history would wake up your history and the anchor that you had for me when I told you that my father, your grandfather was dead. Little did I know that my mother, had told you the truth about that issue, at least her truth in that issue. But let me set the record straight, for years as a little boy I thought that my father had abandoned his two sons and his wife my mother. All I knew was the story that was told by Mary my mother your grandmother and her sister Eleonora and Mike grandmother your great grandmother Florence crake. But because Mary my mother had chosen to leave Mississippi and start out a life of her own, mainly because Joe, my father, really didn't have the drive to do anything except sit drink corn liquor, and gamble. I guess she thought that if there was going to be a break in the family name that she had to do something about it herself and the best thing was to leave Mississippi to leave Alabama and all of those old experiences of discrimination behind. But I remember often she would say to succeed in the world that we live today all Nego's had to be white. I'd really never understood that as a young child until a trip that we took down the Oklahoma somewhere on a plantation, I think I was maybe 10 or 11 years old. My brother RJ has suddenly been whisked up and sent down to the old plantation when he was about save 14 or 15. I thought that was so me because I really missed playing with him and seeing him, and waking up in the morning as he would waive that skillet of frying bacon over my bed to wake me up. But as it turned out he was taken away because he had made a girl in the Kansas City pregnant. And in those days to keep the gossip down the child or the mother or both would be sent away to some far place where no one knew the real truth and when and if they returned sometimes the child that came back with them would be told to us and to the other neighbors, to keep a good name alive, that this was our nephew from down South that was going to live with us now because of some hardship that had taken place down on the plantation. Of course we know now that the woman was named Audrey and the child was named Jean. I wondered why whenever we had family gatherings there was always this little girl that would be brought over to share the talk with and then from the other side of the family we had these other people that will show up LB told these are your cousins, but in those days anybody dark skin was called our cousins. I know this must be somewhat confusing for you but it's the way I remember it I had many many nights and lots of time to sit with a piece of paper and draw out the family while I sat at the fire station as a fireman. The guys at the fire house they would watch TV and said waiting for the fire bell but I was not accepted in the room where they were, because the conversations will always be something derogatory about black people and they would make it obvious to me that they did not want me there but they had to accept me on the team because the chief of the fire department and the mayor said so. I finally discovered that if I went into the TV room first and selected a channel on the television, and sat there in front of it watching whatever it was; that they would never change the station, it was like having to confront me about my choice. When I discovered that I chose to tune the TV station always to the talk new show our classical music. I discovered that most of the firemen that were white light what we called hillbilly music, our country is called now but they did not like to see the talk shows about the news they did not like to see the ballet dancer owner tippy toes, they did not like the tenor singing with the New York Philharmonic. While I had finally found a way to have peace and control so I started my soap education on learning how to talk listening to it would armor and the new shows and any other talk show about any subject that was on one of the stations that broadcast that and only that 24 hours a day well, actually TV did not stay on 24 hours a day usually by 2 AM, the national anthem was played, and TV broadcasting within for the day.

Let me bring in some other facts that may not have been talked about laughingly the the way we used to eat I told you about not having safe food in the refrigerator. But when I was assigned to fire Station number two, which was located in what we called the bottoms, are the industrial district. No one really liked that district because the fires didn't take place nearly as often as they did in residential neighborhoods, but when they did have a fine it was usually always an industrial fire which meant large buildings hot dangerous chemical fires and the like. But in that area were also where all of the truckers and the railroad men would hang out in the evenings, and where they were so was the prostitute, and where the prostitutes were, were the housing the apartments on the second floor over the bars that were scanned it along the street. As an important side note there was one Tavern or eating place called big Mary. I remember she was very happy when she found that number two had a colored fireman, almost like if she had a fire I would be the first one there and perhaps she may have been right because when she heard about the food being tampered, she would fix a special plate and she would walk the block distance down to the firehouse and bring me dinner or lunch. All I had to do was call her on the phone and ask, what's on the menu today. Her language was shall we say colorful, and the reply on the phone would be what the fark do you care it tastes good and you'll eat it whenever I bring. And so it was she would bring it, and I would eat. As time went by the other members of the department at number two, with smell the aromas of this fresh prepared soul food, cornbread, green, beans of all kinds, mashed potatoes, corn, I mean fresh corn on the cop car. Soul it wasn't long before the guys on my shift,

I mean the white ones, would ask me; the you think big Mary would cook me something, if I paid her. Now I became ambassador for food. So they would talk to me, I would call big Mary, she would bring the food after they paid me for in advance laughing of course if the plate was 295, I told them it was four dollars. They paid, I paid big Mary, of course my plate was always free, so I made a little extra money, and actually it made me feel powerful because for the first time down there at number two or any of the integrated firehouses I felt like I had some control. Actually now that I think about it, I was the driver of the damned truck, so their lives were being protected by me driving at high rates of speed siren blaring going to a fire. For the record I never felt like I should or would cause them danger because I almost felt like they were little children that I had to protect as we drove to a fine. Especially when the chief would come to our station and advise that we had to keep the fire truck clean, I mean clean clean. If you remember whenever you would visit a fire station, the wheels, behind the wheels up around the back of the truck under the truck everywhere there was the red truck there was no dirt, there was no mud. And guess who had to inspect the truck to make sure that it was clean everywhere, you know it was me. And believe me if the truck was not going, when the chief came by to inspect, all I had to say was I had to clean it by myself that's why it's still dirty. All hell would break loose then, and no one would get any rest or sleep because the chief would make everybody even the guys in the bed get up pull the truck out front and would have to wash it whether it was rain snow sleet are tornadoes so, after while my word was well if I pointed people jumped the only people that didn't jump, was the chief of the station however very shortly we became fairly good friends I guess if you can have a friend in an integrated fire station. This was my first lesson with how power works, so friend or not, I became a member of the group, if you know what I mean. So as I stated that fire department life got better conversations started and I became the teacher of black culture in the fire station. So many of the guys had no experience with Negroes at all. So almost every day something on television are a sports of activity are sports game on TV I would have questions that was sound something like: why don't your people do this or why do your people do that are how did you come to be able to do that so well things like that. Things kind of condescending but yet it was conversation, it was growth, it was movement toward understanding a race of people that either one of us did not really understand. So for a while I got a nickname," chuckle chuckle", as professor Nichols, because I had learned how to say big words that I had heard on television, so I practiced using them on them." laughing laughing", I'm sure sometimes I use the word the wrong way, but they did know the difference, most of the words they would stare me and then say what is that me, so you see the sun that's really how I learned a lot of these impressive words which were to help me a few years later when we had a black assistant chief of the fire department, which was probably done to attain more federal funds. My mother was extremely pleased because she would bring down some of the Masons that were friends of Mr. Ewing and sit in the day room or the room we played the handball or don't remember the name the little ping-pong that's it played ping-pong and they were set and talk and I think, there were more colored people black people in the room together talking than any of these white guys had ever seen together at one time, in fact the chief asked me one time you mean you guys have meetings and sit talk and laugh and just like we do. It's unbelievable of how the bad information rumors and incorrect things can go through a society that believe that people of a different color or people with a different language can be so different then another set of people. In actuality there is really no difference people that have families raise their children and try to survive pay their bills and enjoy life, isn't this true of all families of all nations all places. In 1978 I came to work one day and the chief of the whole department was at the station when I came on duty. I didn't realize it then but he mentioned a name the same as mine except it was a Junior. He asked me was that my son I proudly answered yes yes it is. I wasn't to know then but later as we talked you were working at the TV station as a weekend stringer, you know finding stories and selling them to the station and that was a mere that was trying to get elected. I believe his name was reared, and as we know now he had no knowledge about how to appeal to the TV camera, you instructed him on how to talk to the camera or make it appear as if there was a group of people and the camera was only one of them on the front steps of City Hall. I found out that this was some of what mother Mary was talking about where she said white Negroes. She did mean we had to change color, she just met we had to merge and impress the people that had power and the people that had power were white. So as we know shortly after that I was promoted to fire inspect. They had never been a black are Negro fire inspector, but it was exceedingly difficult for me. Nobody knew this but I could not write, and really could not read very well either. I'm sure that English teacher that your mother had in school and I had in school and you going to the same high school, Sumner, that teacher named Mrs. Bloodworh is turning in her grave, she tried to teach us how to speak how to write and how to appreciate Edgar Allen whole his works as well as Shakespeare but some work to some stuck some didn't. So with the help of your mother mostly and you, all of my reports and those typed statements of fire investigations were all done at home on the Royal typewriter that had been purchased for you in school. Yeah I know you told me that that was one of the best things that helped you in your school was having to type those reports and understanding how the system really worked. You don't know it brought tears to your grandmother's eyes and once she started crying I would start crying and there we would all sit at the table with tears running down our faces watching you type these reports helping your dad.

So it seems that mother Mary was correct, she was seeing her dream of creating white Negroes, was actually working. She was saying her son and now her grandson began to work outside of the Negro box. The box that meant that all you could do was work on a chain gang, or a street crew, or a job that required no thinking just working your back, your muscles.

You can bet I was really surprised when Haley, member of the Kansas Senate, had worked around to get your mother chosen to be the first female African-American director of nursing on Gov. Bennetts I think I've got that news report some hair here that we can read that cow remember how that was and you don't know, how it made us feel when you became her press secretary, yeah I know you are green and scared as hell, but we all stood back when you made the statements to the press on the front steps of our little house especially with that ruling that took place, you remember about the pro-choice thing and the election with the Senate and governor. Well will have to talk about that in another chapter I guess you are the next chapter at least we thought that you would be the first person in our family that would go to college. My college was the television station listing to the commentators and copying what they said. We were so proud, although you never liked the term, and my mother now gone not living would have been smiling to to know that her legacy, her dream, the train that she put on the track and started for the next generation to become, as she called a white Negro, more successful than any other member of the family.

Down to the station on the bus and would spend several hours with me outside the fire station consoling me, and helping me understand

My place for the advancement of colored people had to be there this was my place my time to take a step up for our children for our community. Hell I remember saying why does it have to be me, there's lots of other Negroes why can't they do it. But as it is, I guess I was chosen, and he was to be me, to be all alone in that environment.

You may remember son, that many times in the summer, you were required to ride your bicycle all the way down to Fairfax from where we lived on Oakland, to bring me lunch.

well dad would you like to start this again, okay okay great what do you want to know, just start where you left off you know back when you did not tell me everything about the guns you know: well as I recall that was the highlight of the time that we spent near this big town in Germany I think it was Bremerhaven our something like that the next big thing I remember was a little town in Wurzburg Germany, and there was a bar that had been bombed and they moved the bar and all the drinks in the wine below ground and out, basement. Space but one of the things that I liked is this big curve to bar went around the whole room almost and GIs could sit down and carved messages in short letters to their girlfriends back home but it would cost you I think a nickel something like that, so of course you know that I carved your mother's name in there and with something like I love naphthalene I was really warm

When you wrote to me and told me you had found that scratching in that bar in Wurzburg I began crying, fortunately I was on watch that night working as a firefighter in Kansas City so no one saw me but it was a very hard night, crying, to realize that life and history had gone full cycle and now my son was in the same place where I had been years earlier. I am sure the reason why you found it so easily is because your mother's name is very unique, NANTHALYNE...

I suppose that's about the only thing I remember that was good about the time that I was in the service that tied us together with the time that you were in Southeast Asia and of course Germany I know that we were really afraid, your mother and I, when we discover that you were not only in German or Europe, that you were also in Southeast Asia. We did ask around a cousin we thought that if you are single surviving son that the military would not put you and I harm's way area where you could be hurt, at least that's what the rules said. But your grandmother Mary said you were different sort of person that I was in the service, and probably you had volunteered to go. Space so when we found out that you had volunteered to go, actually we were quite angry, but still proud just the same. In fact that's where most of our gray hairs came from after we determine, that you were not only in Europe but God knows where else on the world you were. Getting back to my war the days and then weeks in the months seem to go by so slowly, where we we wanted to be home, we wanted to see our good friends, and sleep in a warm bed where I can hear my grandmother frying bacon and making biscuits and inviting me to breakfast on that sunny warm mornings in Kansas. It wasn't long, actually 19th for any form I believe, that we found our way on a big boat once again, on our way back to the United States. I can't tell you how I felt most of the men in my group on the way back we separate ourselves at night, to a corner of our little sleeping area where we silently cried with thankfulness that we had survived, God knows that many of my friends that I remembered in basic training, in Texas, that sailed the ocean with us to France, then drove through Germany and some of the other areas that were no longer with us. It's hard now for me to remember the names but so easy for me to see the faces of these young guys that had come from other homes just like mine, but were not to go back to their homes like we were. The one story that I just remembered that I forgot was the one about the chaplain. I remember we were under fire the enemy, the Germans, were shooting at us from the top of the hill the first let me say we had been hanging around the mess hall tent to get something to eat and it was very quiet so, it seems like whenever it was quiet the chaplain would appear, and he would walk around and with his Bible and and he would talk to us. One of the lines he was say all the time is that we should pray we should be hopeful and we should be thankful. He also stated if ever there is a situation where you're in danger and you are afraid that you might be injured shot of killed. Remember that we have the shield and he would hold up the Bible and wave it around so that we can all see, and he asked us to believe and let the shield protect us. Well then after that somehow we were discovered at a German platoon started shooting at us as the metal bullets would strike the metal pots and pans of the mess hall everybody got to the ground, and the chaplain, and his driver, immediately ran for their Jeep. Starting the Jeep they quickly made a U-turn and off they went down the dusty road way and out the little knoll mountainous strip of muddy road and one of my friends, that was in our Negro brigade managed to stand up by side a tree, and he shouted to the chaplain, come back come back you took the shield bring back the shield. Even though our lives where before our faces with bullets flying all around, you can hear the roar of laughter from the battalion commander the platoon and some of the other men as we scrambled to get below behind in any kinda shelter we had... we still laugh about that, whenever I talk to some of the survivors of opportunity on the phone that's one thing we can never forget. Space I tried telling that joke to the Rev. of your church here in Seattle, but... I don't think he thought it was funny. Well jumping ahead again back to the boat we soon reached the dock in New York City we passed by the Statue of Liberty, then this island mass, don't remember what it was called, but we can see American made cars. No jeeps no tanks just people milling around on this ferryboat that was going past us, with kids and women, that I mentioned women, of course I did, staring up at this big huge boat that all of these military people were out on the deck on the rails, hanging over waving whatever we had in our hands. Even thou it warms my heart to recall that we were back home, back to the US. Some of us openly cried, because you know, men are really supposed to cry. Then it was the long trip on the train to get back the Kansas City, it seemed like it took longer on the train to get home, then it did to sail across the ocean, which I might add is a lot of days on water, on the waves up and the waves down in the wind and the rain and the uncertainty of will this thing get us home or could we be sunk in the middle of this great wide water ocean as I recall, it was scary especially two men who had never been on a boat much less to another country.

But finally we got home; it was 1943, my family my mother and my girlfriend was so glad to see us and the food... we had was just wonderful I, mean, real food, I mean food cooked by the hands of people who knew how to cook. No frozen peas corn okra coming out of a can lightly salted and boiled in water served on a tinplate with the bread that smelled like the very can that it came from. I mean we may have to go out tonight to get some fried chicken my favorite catfish, and you know the kind of cooking that you grew up with with your grandmother loving to be at the stove, and loving the looks on our faces as we consumed everything that she put on the table not to mention the blueberry pie, I guess I better stop laughing, here because I'm getting hungry.

The happiness soon left the, as soon as we removed our uniforms, which we wore almost every day for about two weeks. During this time whenever we walked downtown, there were pats on the back, smiled and well-wishers telling us thank you for serving and more. But as you know all good things must come to an end soon or later it was too soon for us, when I was walking downtown with my mother uniforms were off, we were now in plain clothes, and some guy walking down the street wanted me to step off the curb to allow him to pass. Of course with my newfound patriotism and believe that now we can now be true men and citizens since we had projected our lives and our hopes and to the democracy called America, but it wasn't to be so, when the younger white man said hey, don't you know Negroes are supposed to get off the sidewalk to get out of our way. I was so angry and refusing to move off the sidewalk I stepped up ready to punch his eyes out. But my mother in her infinite wisdom grabbed my arm and told me, it's okay sugar it's okay. I recall the long walk home in the ride on the bus of course sitting in the rear section. Although in Kansas City it really wasn't required and there was no sign on the bus, that told us we had to sit in a certain section. It was thought of expected that if you lived there, that you knew your proper place, and you respected the other people of your race, as to not make trouble for. Now you must remember, that I've been away from the city dodging bullets, martyrs, and enemy snipers: even though I didn't have my shield: to protect us from those flying pieces of metal.

Let me mention another important part of my life as a man as a soldier and now as a father because in June 1945 my wife and I had our first son, Brandon Junior. Everybody in the family on both sides, seem to carry flags of joy because on your mother's side on my wife's there had not been a male child born and almost 2 generations. So obviously they, seem to be forefront in spoiling our first son with all kinds of gifts, baby beds, wagons, rollways, you name it: you had it. This was the first time that the other side of our family are my family which had passed and were known to be white; actually came over to our part of town to visit and to play with my male child. Also for the first time, I was receiving many tips from the elderly members of all sides of both families, of how to raise a child are in the words of your great grandmother how are we going to raise a white Negron. I know that sounds funny now, but in those days, anyone that had a child who was light skinned was considered to be fortunate. It was thought that if you were light, you would have more possibilities of success, and happy life because you were closer to blending in the status quo, or those who had power or, those that would have power in the future. In that day all Negroes had hopes of better things, freedom, jobs, and money to live a life for them and their children that would far exceed anything that black folk had ever imagined what happened in their lives.

As you grew as a little baby, we stayed at my mother's house. Out in that area of Kansas City that was call rattle bone hollow. Officially it was called when Darrell, and so as history shows just across the way from where we were living on fifth Street, and the Quintero area and the Indians name us, was another county which very rich Jewish people live, and as it was said part of the Underground Railroad came right through that area. In close circles, and at times when no one was listening, the conversations on the front porches and at the city park at family gatherings talked about this very often, as some of our family and some of our friends of our families had actually escaped their bondage years earlier, from the South, as they use the Underground Railroad to migrate further North from the southern states.

Being back in Kansas City, at home, I was still considered to be a lofty black American as was, my brother RJ who had also joined the military and had decided to stay in the military, and make it his career. As many brothers we did not agree. So he continued to be a soldier, and I went looking for work. Every day I was reminded by my mother and other members of the family, you got a boy now so you got a work, and you've got a bring him up right. I had various jobs from family milling company I worked at Griffin wheel boundary those of the guys that make the wheels for trains you know those big metal things that go on railroad train. Then I got a real good job at Owens Corning Fiberglas and about that same time your mother and I purchased our first house, on Oakland. It was a duplex and the family next door that rented from house named kitchen, had a young man named Billy. Billy had a developmental problem and really although he was a big guy, his age never exceeded more than nine years old. But he became your favorite play buddy, simply because he was right next door. In 1951 or so, the neighbor next door told us of an opening at the General Motors assembly plant, down in Fairfax. That was considered to be a really good job at the time for any Negroes that really wanted to work hard, and I did. As I recall we bought our first car right after we bought the duplex. It was a 51 Chevrolet green notch. Your mother learned how to drive, because she would take me to work early in the morning, and keep the car all day so that she could take you to your grandmother's while she went to work as a seamstress, making bowling shirts. She and your aunt Shirley had great jobs during the war, at the Pratt and Whitney plant making engines for the US Army bombers. But as all things happen, when the war ended so did the jobs, especially the women since all of the men now were returning. In those jobs were reserved for men that returned from the war, and that meant now many women were an important. My mother Mary had left my blood father when she moved up to Kansas from Mississippi. For years I thought that my father had ran away on my mother but it was to be many many years, before I would discover that actually it was the other way around. Mama had high hopes on what I could become and her children's children could become an thought that it be best if she left to go to a more progressive area of the world to raise her children. So on the freight train RJ Vernon and Mary, traveled of the rail line until RJ, got so sick that she had to get off. And as I'm told that just happened to be in the train district of Fairfax Kansas. As the story goes, she walked up the big Quintero Hill on a cool evening. Getting about halfway up the Hill and not knowing where she was going to sleep a put us down to rest a lady up about 15 stairs holler down to her and said, now where is you going. I'm told my mother shouted back I'm going to my house at the top of the hill. The lady, whose name was Beulah, shouted back you ain't going out there to know house because a no colors up that high on the hill. So come on up here and bring those kids with you. It was to be that we would live there for a year, and my mother would work in the same business that Buehler was an, which was the laundry. Now mother never told us all the details except for some reason, she had a boyfriend, named Mr. Jenkins. And shortly after meeting him we moved up the top of the hill on fifth Street and our own house, and a few years after that we moved down to the middle of Kansas City Kansas, on a street called land. Now you have to remember some of these facts are kind of old for me, and may not be totally accurate but I remember Mr. Jenkins died or left when I was kind a young it was before I went to the military. So while I was in the military mother had no one except her mother who moved in to help her with bells cleaning and cooking that was your grandmother Craig, and the other side of the family, which everybody knew or at least thought they were white. So now I'm back from the service and I married, have a child, have a good job at VOP plant, that's Buick Oldsmobile Pontiac plant. And my mother married she was a member of the I think they called it the rising Star. Space in any case that organization was kind of the ladies of the Masonic Lodge. Her new boyfriend was Mr. Ewing, a real dark skinned man, and a high-ranking member of the local Masons, don't remember what number it was: but he was pretty high up there. In about 1956 the city of Kansas City, had a chance to get large sum of money from the federal government, that would be used to buy new fire trucks and build some new fire stations throughout the city. But one of the provisos was, that some of the men who were firemen and policemen had to be Negroes. For the next four years are so, the city recruited several Negro staff for the fire department, the police department, and the city work crews to fix the streets, and clear the snow during the winter. I don't have all the facts but shortly after 1959, the city was trying to purchase new fire trucks, because the ones we had, named the law fronds were given to the city from Europe and were used, that is to say they were not new. And of course the old fire horses were given to the part of the city with the most minorities, Negroes and the Mexicans, oh and don't let me forget the poor whites. So once again in order to get the new fire engines and the money for the new equipment for law enforcement, the city was forced to integrate the public servants. In those days the powerful Negroes in the city always belonged to the Masons, and since my mother was the girlfriend of one of the top Masons: guess what. They apparently needed some fresh drivers to help integrate the department and my lucky break, I had certification from the federal government, US Army, that I was a truck driver covering several different sizes of vehicles. So came the dream job offer. I can join a different section of the fire department and be one of the first truck drivers ever to drive a truck like that any way, for the city. We were so happy until we discovered that instead of having all of the Negros firemen at two stations, that were located in the black neighborhoods, that we were to be dispersed throughout the wind that County city of Kansas City fire departments. That actually meant one Negro for each fire station in the city. Unbeknownst to me this was to be worse than my time in Europe and the service. Most of the fire department at that time. In Kansas City were people that were Slavic background there was lots of talk about they were pulled a tip some men I can't spell it but it's a kind of bread that a lot of Slavic's would make for their families. My mother, and never let me forget that this was a job then be white people would love to have, but I had it, and I had to support that son born 47 and this would be the best way to do that.

The working shift for a fireman was at that time, four days on, and two days off. So we slept at the station for at least three nights, and prepared our food in the kitchen, and our groceries in the refrigerator. I quickly found that there was only one section in the refrigerator that I was allowed to have my groceries. It was in the crisper section down below. I actually remember the name of the

Frigidaire was a shell the Nader can't spell it, but I remember it and there, I kept all my sandwiches bread and everything that I was to eat including soup. But because of the hate of some of the people that I was working around, who were white, I soon found that many of my sandwiches had been tainted with human waste, and my Tea or Kool-Aid always had a strange smell which resembled urine. Of course I reported this to the chief, who simply told me, this is a new thing for many people, you're just going to have to grin and bear it. Many times I really wanted to take a weapon, and just hit everybody in the head at that station, and then walk out, catch the bus and go home. Once again my mother Mary, seem like she could tell when things were going bad because, she would bring my lunch every day during the summer. I know from your complaints, that you thought that was just crazy. But the real reason was the only way that I could have a healthy lunch and dinner, was to have someone bring my food in daily. I found out later after talking to many of the other black firemen, that we got to know, that everybody had the same problem throughout the city and had their families friends etc. bring them food in lockboxes that were not perishable; that could stay outside sometimes in the kitchen, a locker with a lock on it, that cannot be tampered. No, I didn't tell you that either. Because at that time, your age you noticed everything, it would affect your thinking, this would only cause you to have hate for anybody white, and if you remember you had just gotten about two friends that were white, poor but white.

I really thought that to you might start a growing hate inside for different people. I really wanted you to judge people for what they are, not from general predujes.

That kind of behavior continued for several years, and those of us that were members of the integration, just kept our mouths shut, and waited for the day that we could improve that. Even Mr. Ewing, who was responsible for me actually getting the job suggested that we be happy where we were, and look forward to the next jump in rank. Actually I thought that this was the top, we would never go any higher, but I was grateful, that my son could see me at least, in a decent job, as a public servant.... when I came home I didn't have to leave my greasy glass infested clothing out on the front steps anymore, to keep those dangerous chemicals away from you. Now... I don't want you to forget that my mother, your grandmother, from the very first, when you were a baby, always reminded us that we had to be a different kind of Negro, as she called it, a white negga, she used to say. I really never understood what she meant until one day, we were sitting on the front porch at the house on Oakland. You remember the one that was partially built, we purchased and moved into it in about 1960. I think it was our first year living there in the yellow house on the hill, and you and your friend, were cutting grass for the older members of the neighborhood that couldn't cut their own, although you never really wanted to do it; this was something that we just did to make our neighborhood look good. As my mother had taught me you always take care of the neighbor on either side of your house, and if everybody did that in the whole neighborhood, then the whole neighborhood would remain clean and neat, and so it was. Ok ok I ramble do recall one of the boys stayed on the corner in the summer time with his aunt, Mrs. Anderson. You know the **big** white house on the corner. Mrs. Anderson was the sister of Haley family. One of the Haley's went on to become the first black senator, for the state of Kansas. His brother Alex, stayed in the military for his career, and it was he, Mr Alex Haley, who wrote roots. This block on Everett was an interesting block, because everybody that lived on this block was black,or as we said then Negro, All of us had a job that was supposed to be the upper crust of the Negro community. Down near the one end of the block we had a postman, who was third in command for the local postal offices, and then we had several other people who were executives that the Kansas Call paper, the only Negro paper in town, then there was Mr. Lewis, who was the Negro superintendent of schools, the negro schools, and across the Street him, Halo he was the head teacher of the music department for the greater Kansas City schools. At least the Negro portion of the school system, that was allowed by Mr. Slagle, FL Slagle. as I recall he allowed for the black schools, oops, the Negro schools to have their own separate board of education, you know the old phrase separate but equal. But let's go back to sitting on the front porch of the Anderson home on the corner while you listened to Alex Haley. He read from little notes and scripts that he had from his travels, talking about his family. Little did we know then , in years to come, that Alex would have a book written, read, and made into a movie. That movie as you remember was called roots, and became a bestseller, and a highly rated movie about Negro culture. That was about the same time that you ask me where was your grandfather, or where was my daddy. I never knew that listening to someone else's history would wake up your need for history. The anger that you had for me, when I told you that my father, your grandfather was dead. Little did I know that my mother, had told you the truth about that issue, at least her truth in that issue. Let me set the record straight, for years as a little boy I thought that my father had abandoned his two sons and his wife, my mother. All I knew was the story that was told by my mother, your grandmother. Her sister Eleonora, and My grandmother, your great grandmother Florence Craig always filled in the emotional truth. Because mother had chosen to leave Mississippi and start out a life of her own, Joe, my father, really didn't have the drive to do anything except, sit drink corn liquor, and gamble. I guess she thought that if there was going to be a break in the family name, that she had to do something about it herself. The best thing was to leave Mississippi, to leave Alabama and all of those old experiences of discrimination behind. But I remember often she would say to succeed in the world, that we had to blend; we Negro's had to blend with white. I'd really never understood that as a young child, until a trip that we took down the Oklahoma somewhere on a plantation, I think I was maybe 10 or 11 years old. My brother RJ has suddenly been whisked up and sent down to the old plantation when he was about save 14 or 15. I thought that was so mean, because I really missed playing and seeing him. We were waking up in the morning and he would waive that skillet of frying bacon over my bed to wake me up. But as it turned out, he was taken away because he had made a girl in Kansas City pregnant. In those days, to keep the gossip down; the child or the mother or both, would be sent away to some far place where no one knew the real truth. When and if they returned... sometimes the child that came back with them would be called our cousin or anything that the neighbors would believe, to keep a good name alive, . Of course we know now that the woman was named Audrey and the child was named Jean. I wondered why whenever we had family gatherings there was always this little girl that would be brought over to share food. The lie was told that he or she was from the other side of the family. Other people would show up , these are your cousins they would say, but in those days anybody dark skin was called our cousins. I know this must be somewhat confusing for you, but it's the way I remember it. I had many many nights and lots of time to sit with a piece of paper and draw out the family while I sat at the fire station as a fireman.

The guys at the fire house, they would watch TV , waiting for the fire bell, but I was not accepted in the room where they were, because the conversations were always be something derogatory about black people. They would make it obvious that they did not want me there. They had to accept me on the team because the mayor and chief of the fire department said so. Finally discovered that if I went into the TV room first, and selected a channel on the television, and sat there in front of it watching whatever it was; that they would never change the station, it was like having to confront me about my choice. When I discovered that... WOW, I chose to tune the TV station always to the talk or news show our classical music program, on the educational channel. I discovered that most of the firemen were not lovers of classical music, they liked hillbilly country or blue grass music They did not like to see the talk shows about the news or politic its ,they did not like to see the ballet dancer on her tippy toes, they did not like the tenor singing with the New York Philharmonic. I had finally found a way to have peace and control so I started my visual classics education, learning how to talk listening to the news shows and any other talk show about any subject that was on one of the stations that broadcast only that 24 hours a day well, actually TV did not stay on 24 hours a day usually by 2 AM the national anthem was played, and TV broadcasting was off for the day.

Let me bring in some other facts that may not have been talked about laughingly the the way we used to eat I told you about not having safe food in the refrigerator. But when I was assigned to fire Station number two, which was located in what we called the bottoms, or the industrial district. No one really liked that district because the fires didn't take place as often as they did in residential neighborhoods, boring station house, but when they did have a fire it was always an industrial fire, which meant large buildings, hot dangerous chemical fires and the like. But in that area was also where all of the truckers and the railroad men would hang out in the evenings, and where they were, so was the prostitute, and where the prostitutes were, were the housing the apartments on the second floor over the bars, that were littered along the street. As an important side note, there was one Tavern or eating place called big Mary's. I remember she was extremely happy when she found that number two had a colored fireman, she would fix a special plate, she would walk the block distance down to the firehouse and bring me dinner or lunch. All I had to do was call her on the phone and ask, what's on the menu today. Her language was shall we say colorful, and the reply on the phone would be, what the fuck do you care, it tastes good and you'll eat whenever I bring. So she would bring it, and I would eat it. As time went by the other white men at number two, would smell the aromas of this freshly prepared soul food, cornbread, green, beans of all kinds, mashed potatoes, corn, I mean fresh corn on the cob. So ...ul it wasn't long before the guys on my shift, I mean the white ones, would ask me; the you think big Mary would cook me something, if I paid her. Now I became ambassador for food. So they would talk to me, I would call big Mary, she would bring the food after they paid me for in advance laughing of course if the plate was 295, I told them it was four dollars. They paid, I paid big Mary, of course my plate was always free, so I made a little extra money, actually it made me feel powerful, because for the first time down there at number two or any of the integrated firehouses I felt like I had some control. Actually now that I think about it, I was the driver of the damned truck, so their lives were being protected by me, driving at high rates of speed siren blaring going to a fire. For the record I never felt like I should or would cause them danger, because I almost felt like they were little children that I had to protect, as we drove to a fire. Especially when the chief would come to our station and advise that we had to keep the fire truck clean, I mean clean clean. If you remember, whenever you would visit a fire station, the wheels, behind the wheels up around the back of the truck under the truck everywhere there was the red truck there was no dirt, there was no mud. And guess who had to inspect the truck to make sure that it was clean everywhere, you know it it was me, the driver. I was responsible for the truck. And believe me if the truck was not glowing, when the chief came by to inspect, all I had to say, I had to clean it by myself that's why it's still dirty. All hell would break loose then, and no one would get any rest or sleep because the chief would make everybody even the guys in the bed get up, pull the truck out front and would have to wash it whether it was rain snow sleet are tornadoes so, after a while, my word was well…. If I pointed, people jumped, the only people that didn't jump, was the chief of the station, however very shortly we became fairly good friends. I guess if you can have a friend in an integrated fire station. This was my first lesson with how power works, so friend or not, I became a member of the group, if you know what I mean. So as I stated the fire department life got better; conversations started and I became the teacher of black culture in the fire station. So many of the guys had no experience with Negroes at all. So almost every day something on television or a sports of activity are sports game on TV I would have questions that would sound something like: why don't your people do this or why do your people do that, or how did you come to be able to do that so well, things like that. Things kind of condescending, but yet it was conversation, it was growth, it was movement toward understanding a race of people that either one of us did not really understand. So for a while I got a nickname chuckle chuckle as professor Nichols, because I had learned how to say big words that I had heard on television, so I practiced using them on them   laughing laughing. I'm sure sometimes I use the word the wrong way, but they did know the difference, most of the words they would stare me. and then say what is that me, so you see the son, that's really how I learned a lot of these impressive words , which were to help me a few years later, when we had a black assistant chief of the fire department, which was probably done to attain more federal funds. My mother was extremely pleased because she would bring down some of the Masons that were friends of Mr. Ewing and sit in the day room or the room we played the handball or don't remember the name the little ping-pong that's it played ping-pong and they were set and talk and I think, there were more colored people black people in the room together talking than any of these white guys had ever seen together at one time, in fact the chief asked me one time you mean you guys have meetings and sit talk and laugh and just like we do. It's unbelievable of how the bad information rumors and incorrect things can go through a society that believe that people of a different color or people with a different language can be so different, than another set of people. In actuality there is really, no difference in people; have families raise their children and try to survive, pay their bills and enjoy life, isn't this true of all families of all nations all places. In 1978 I came to work one day and the chief of the whole department was at the station when I came on duty. I didn't realize it then, but he mentioned a name the same as mine except it was a Junior. He asked me was that my son,

I proudly answered yes yes it is. I wasn't to know then but later, as we talked you were working at the TV station as a weekend stringer, you know finding stories and selling them to the station, there was a man that was trying to get elected mayor. I believe his name was Reardon, and as we know now he had no knowledge about how to appeal to the TV camera, you instructed him on how to talk to the camera or make it appear as if there was a group of people, and the camera was only one of them on the front steps of City Hall. I found out that this was some of what mother Mary was talking about, where she said white Negroes. She did not mean we had to change color, she just meant we had to merge and impress the people that had power, and the people that had power were white. So as we know shortly after that I was promoted to fire inspector. They had never been a black are Negro fire inspector, but it was exceedingly difficult for me. Nobody knew this, but I could not write, and really could not read very well either. I'm sure that English teacher that your mother had in school, named Mrs. bloodworh is turning in her grave, she tried to teach us how to speak how to write and how to appreciate, Edgar Allen Poe, his works as well as Shakespeare, some stuck some didn't. So with the help of your mother mostly and you, all of my reports and those typed statements of fire investigations were all done at home on the Royal typewriter that had been purchased for you in school. Yeah I know you told me that that was one of the best things that helped you in your school, was having to type those reports and understanding how the system really worked. You don't know it brought tears to your grandmother's eyes, and once she started crying I would start crying and there we would all sit at the table with tears running down our faces watching you type these reports helping your dad.

So it seems that mother Mary was correct, she was seeing her dream of creating white Negroes, was actually working. She was saying her son and now her grandson began to work outside of the Negro box. The box that meant that all you could do was work on a chain gang, or a street crew, or a job that required no thinking just working your back, your muscles.

You can bet I was really surprised when Haley, member of the Kansas Senate, had worked around to get your mother chosen to be the first female African-American director of nursing for Gov. Bennett's

 I think I've got that news report somewhere here that we can read. I remember now , you don't know, how it made us feel when you became her press secretary, yeah I know you were green, and scared as hell, but we all stood back when you made the statements to the press on the front steps of our little house; especially with that ruling that took place, you remember about the pro-choice thing, and the election with the Senate and governor. We will have to talk about that in another chapter I guess, you are the next chapter at least we thought that you would be the first person in our family that would go to college. My college was the television station listing to the commentators and copying what they said. We were so proud, although you never liked the term, and my mother now gone, not living; She would be smiling to know that her legacy, her dream, the train that she put on the track, next generation to become, as she called a white Negro, more successful than any other member of the family.

So it was a terrible time, and grandma died, I I think I was living over at the house on Grandview, so you heard her talk longer about things she wished for family, glad that you think that she would be very proud, she always seemed to love me a lot and let me get away with almost everything. (sr)Yes she did, your grandmother really loves you a lot and she saw you more than RJ's. he had no children she could touch, put her hand on; you know, like Jean, she wasn't around, so she Felt that she had to love one of the children, so it became you, you were close and you soaked up everything you could from grandma. (jr) Yes I did I I I love my Grandna, as I called her (sr) So son, when you left to go to college what happened. we never knew what you were going through, as a result of our training, and our money ,laughing, well, (jr) dad I thought because I knew, that you would know that It was a traumatic time for me. You and mom drove me down to Kansas State College of Pittsburgh, a big town,(laughing) and we drove up to the dorm, actually it was more of ah oh, I don't know hotel condo arrangement that I had been put in, I didn't know that there were very few African-American, called young blacks, that were on the campus. I think I counted somewhere around 10 people of color, and some of those I found were not really African-Americans, what we called ourselves, some were East Indian, and one guy was from Peru. So the room that I was put in, as you remember, you brought my bags and bags and bags of stuff that mother had packed for every contingency under the sun. Rain weather snow nuclear attack. That black footlocker, and those suitcases. I mean actually I didn't want to hurt her feelings, but after you guys left I picked out about two units of clothes, other than my underwear, so I wore pretty much those black jenes and a red blue green and black madras tie-dyed type shirt, and those black flat tennis shoes. It was easy to weair, and I didn't have to think about anything, about what batched either one of those combinations would match each other, and I was comfortable. But I do remember when we first came upstairs we were there first remember, then this lady an older man but older white, and his son walked up the stairs. The lady, looked at me and said, oh great!! Some boys to help with the bags, boy could you guys go down in our car downstairs, the station wagon, and help get our bags. I recall you glared at her, as I went bouncing down the stairs to help bring the bags up, this was my new new roommate. Steve, was his name a blonde haired bluish gray eyed thin waisted 5'9" white boy. He thought that I was simply helping for the college, but when the parents left, and I picked a bed that I wanted, he then said, is this i your room too, yeah, I said, this is my room too, so I guess we got to be together. the lady, his mom, started gathering up all his valuables stuck them in an over the bed in thenext room, where there were two twin beds.dad I had now reached the front door upstairs laughing. At that point he sat in one part of the room I sat on the other side, next to my portable record player. You know, the one that Grandna had given me, and a few boxes of records that I brought with me. For about an hour we never spoke, he just sat there and when I motioned toward him to look at the records, it was like I had the plague; as he drove backwards, and almost fell off the chair afraid of my gestures. Then I realized that I had a sort of power, much like the power you had at the fire station. The power to have the room solely to yourself, but that proved to be lonely after the first day, with no conversation, no handshake, and no I contact at all. He avoided me like the plague, as he selected his bed in the back room, where they were two beds. Obviously I was to sleep out in the open area, which I preferred anyway because, you had a bigger bed and a window that I can look out across part of the campus. The back bedroom where he chose had no windows only a skylight. It was fine for me that he thought he was in a private room, but then, the door flies open and walks in this lanky white boy, Steve opened the bedroom door and smilingly walked out and said hi guy. And the lanky white guy said I'm John and I see you other two are here so I'm the third roommate. Steve walked over toward him with almost arms in stretched out, like saying thank God there's a white boy with me. He never looked at me but John as he walked toward him John open his arms Steve moved right in for this brotherly hug. As John now really held him tightly, Steve started to backup and let go, and John continued to hold him, like playing a prank on a little brother. After about a minute of this laughing, the look on Steve's face was somewhat alarming. As John looked down at me, sitting on the couch, and. Finally Steve pulled away, as John said, I hope you are sleeping in the room with me, because we're going to have some fun. Steve's face turned bright red actually, his nose looked

like Rudolph the red nosed reindeer. At that point John clumped into the back room with his single bag and threw it on the bed like a soider. It was the bed Steve had chosen, which was closer to the bathroom. Steve quietly said, that's my bed. John spoke up like a football player, and said it used to be, but move your shit, this is mine now. As he clumped in the living room, he extended his hand and said, how are you doing brother. I greeted him with a warm UH UH feeling, but not sure where he was coming from. As you know,dad, that you told me and taught me that sometimes white people will appear warm and friendly, but watch your back. But now I had become a diplomat, because as he left to go down and tell his parents goodbye, Steve approached me and said, what you think about that guy he seems to be very forward. I couldn't help myself, I said, yeah, and I think he really likes you. Once again the red face grew, as he sat on the couch bed next to me, actually so close that it made me nervous. In a few moments Steve came back and said while, I guess I really made you nervous, you are stll reder than red, whats was your name again, Steve uttered the name Steve, and he said I was here second so I get to pick the second band and things like that. John said where you from, Steve said, I'm from Shawnee Mission Kansas. John swung around and said that's the reason. Steve said, the reason for what with a stutter. I'm from overland park, the place where the poor white people live. And you are from the area where the rich white people live. He turned to me and says soul, where are you from brother. I said Wyandotte County Kansas. John smiled and told me, yeah you guys kicked our butts every year and basketball and football, you must be from Sumner, that all black school. I said, yes, that's the school I went to but, I don't play football, I was just in the band and the photography class. John said no matter, you got soul and a bunch of things I wish I had. Then I really thought. this is going to be fun, I felt really relaxed,   but guarded, and wanted to see what the next few days would hold. So grandma raised us to be white, I don't know how far to go, what really not to say, and just to start researching; just what kind of people that I had. I actually thought that Steve was probably an aristocratic homosexual of some kind. And John was a he-man, football, soon to be in the Marines or something like that, just by the way he walked.
 Back to the college. college started and I went to my first class which was electronics, I realized, looking around the room that nobody in the class looked like the, nobody. I thought, here I go again setting the stage and getting all these questions. That was true because the next few times in class, where we had time to talk I was ganged, like I was something odd, and each question was something about, about music, about our football team, and how good at basketball I was. Shamefully, even though I was 6 foot tall and only 165 pounds, I may have looked like a big basketball jock, but the truth is I couldn't play basketball very well... If I could go back in this taping, you probably knew that, watching me trying to play basketball, in the backyard with the basketball goal that you and uncle James installed. I also noticed that in the electronics class, there was no girls, darn, one of the things I want to do first, way away from home, and have a free reign on doing and saying anything I wanted with the ladies. There were no legs, I thought to myself where are they, there's got to be some girls here that I can impress play with, something like that. As you know, and I wrote back home to you and mom, that about a week had gone by and I did find that there was a small complement of black students who met together, usually who met in the cafeteria where I discovered the most scrumptious delicious apple crumb pie I ever had. I never told mom because I

told her that her pie was the best and, I didn't want to start any trouble my first year in college, especially before you guys sent the first tuition check. Steve became closer to me, and John tried to also, it was like I was a prize piece of fruit, and both wanted to be close to me. When I played my music which was obviously soul type of the 1960s, John could sing the words the most of the songs, where Steve could not. really all he knew how to sing was John Croce and the mamas and the popas or the Beatles. They were just recently on the scene about that year. More importantly the college, in the band which I joined and the symphonic orchestra I also joined, there was no other dark skin people at all there either. I decided that I would either learn how to cope, as grandma had told us, or I would just have to feel uncomfortable but, I must go on and I did. I'm sure the one thing that you regret, was my discovery of the motorcycle. It was those little small Honda things that, downtown Pittsburg cycles could be rented. I hung around there waiting for the time that I can rent one. On the campus I started army ROTC. That was a big jump, because once again there was nobody that looked like me. But after a very short time I realize that not only could I do things that others couldn't, because remember the Boy Scout troop, that we had at the church, and the Cub Scouts that mother ran. The scout master, an army drill sergent in the Koren war, taught us how to march, and other military stuff. I knew how to do most of those things,guys in class did not know how to do, I became very well known to the lieutenants in the sergeants running the ROTC program. Most of the little tests that they had, I could pass handily without any stress, because I've seen it all before. Then came then came the parties, and there was my downfall. Outside of town in Pittsburg Kansas, they had strip coal mining,coal strip pit mining. That's where they got coal from just below the surface. they would dig it off the surface, it sat there readily for anyone to take. And after they would strip the coal out of these pits, only about 12 feet deep, and maybe 200 feet diameter; they would simply leave the mounds of dirt around the hole take the coal, and I guess they moved on, because, there were several places where there were five or six holes with dirt around them coal gone and water, would form to make a group of small little lakes. Of course with a little beer and a little Fire they became hiding places where all kinds of things would go on, but the girls were there in their wonderful Splenda. I could stay there at a party, and ultimately drink free beer,stolen from some frat house on campus, that would be provided if we let some of the frat boys play with our girls, and the girls would get loose and so what we. Didn't have to worry about curfew, because we were not in the dorms, and I had a room key, and I could sneak into the unit without bothering the two guys in the back. No one would know what time I came in, do they care, so this one on the first semester; until I got my grades. Band was fine, ROTC was fine, but my basic courses, they were terrible, and after a week or so the Dean, called me into his office, to report to me that I wasn't doing very good, if I didn't improve I might be seen as a colored academic this disgrace. He said we only let a few of you boys in this school.. and you are messing up things for your kind.

NEXT CHAPTER, I guess I will need to grow up

www.ingramcontent.com/pod-product-compliance
Lightning Source LLC
Chambersburg PA
CBHW060644030426
42337CB00018B/3435